CH00664263

50

Inspiring

Iranian

Women

تقدیم به نخبما بساری
یکی از حقوقدانان و زنان برجسته ایران عزیزمان
به مناسبت سالروز تولد ایشان
(به سفارش خشایار جی رید مارس ۲۰۲۱)

Roshi Rouzbehani

Roshi

Copyright ©2020 Roshi Rouzbehani

All right reserved. No part of this book may be reproduced or used in any manner without the prior written permission of the copyright owner, except for the use of quotations in a book review.

First published in 2020

Printed by Biddles Ltd
King's Lynn
Norfolk
PE32 1SF

ISBN 978-1-913663-41-4

Please visit www.RoshiRouzbehani.com

Contents

Introduction

While there has been recent interest in celebrating the life and work of remarkable women from around the world, I do not believe Iranian women have received the recognition they deserve. That is why I decided to use my art to pay tribute to 50 inspiring women from my country. Admittedly, one of the most challenging aspects of this project was to limit myself to only 50 individuals from a long list of Iranian women who have made meaningful contributions to the arts, sciences, sports, education and philanthropy.

This book portrays and celebrates these 50 astounding women from Iran who have made great strides in their professional lives despite the dominant patriarchal social norms. The mini-biographies highlight the character and achievements of these women while the illustrations—done in my unique style—can hopefully serve as a modern touch on how we picture each of them.

As an Iranian woman, I am honoured to introduce and highlight these extraordinary women who form an essential part of my cultural heritage. As an illustrator, I am excited to illustrate these admirable women to make the book fun, colourful, engaging and accessible to all ages. To emphasize the Iranian heritage of these incredible women, for each portrait, I have designed borders inspired by decorative frames found in Persian miniature paintings.

I hope this book sheds light on these inspiring women and their remarkable achievements alongside all the disparities, obstacles and limitations they faced. Beyond this, I hope this book challenges some of the stereotypes that may exist about Iranian women and serve as a source of inspiration for anyone, of any age, anywhere in the world, to realize their dreams and ambitions.

This book is dedicated to my mom, Nahid, for being such a wonderful source of inspiration and for supporting me with her unconditional love.

Activism

Mahlagha Mallah

Mahlagha Mallah (b. 1917), known as the "mother of Iran's nature" is the first female environmental activist and a pioneer in the environmental movements in Iran.

Born and raised in a prominent family, Mahlagha is the granddaughter of BibiKhanum Astarabadi, a remarkable writer, satirist, and women's rights activist, and the daughter of Khadijeh Afzal Vaziri, the girls' education activist and essayist.

In 1993, she and her husband founded the first environmental protection association in Iran focusing on research and educational activities called "Women's Society Against Environmental Pollution," motivated by the desire for "a green Earth and blue Sky."

Now 103 years old, Mahlagha is still passionately engaged in the campaign to raise awareness about environmental issues in Iran.

Mehrangiz Manouchehrian

Mehrangiz Manouchehrian (1906-2000) was a feminist university teacher who championed the struggle for women's rights and played an important role in women's suffrage in Iran.

As one of the first female Iranian lawyers—and later, senator—Mehrangiz was involved in drafting a set of laws extending women's rights in marriage, known as the Family Protection Act.

In 1968, Mehrangiz became the first Iranian to receive the United Nations Prize in the Field of Human Rights for her contributions to the promotion and protection of women's rights.

Noushin Ahmadi Khorasani

Noushin Ahmadi Khorasani (b. 1969) is a women's rights activist, journalist, writer and translator, and a leading figure in the Iranian women's movement.

She is one of the founding members of the One Million Signatures Campaign (2006), a petition to change discriminatory laws against women in Iran. She is also a founder of the Women's Cultural Center (2001-2007), the first NGO created after the Islamic Revolution to focus on women's health and legal issues. In addition, she founded and is editor-in-chief of the Feminist School website, an online resource for women's issues.

Noushin has also written several books and articles about the women's movement in Iran. In 1998, she produced the first Iranian Women's Calendar to introduce and celebrate groundbreaking Iranian women throughout history. Later, in 2009, she published in English a similar calendar called "Iranian Women Who Dare."

Shahla Sherkat

Shahla Sherkat (b. 1956) is a journalist and feminist author as well as one of the pioneers of the women's rights movement in Iran.

In 1991 she founded the monthly magazine *Zanan* (*Women*), the first independent journal established after the Iranian Revolution to focus on feminism and women's rights. The magazine came under fire from the government for its views, and after being suspended for several years and restarting, finally ceased operation in 2015.

In 2005, Shahla was the first Iranian to win The Courage in Journalism Award from the International Women's Media Foundation (IWMF). She also won the Louis Lyons Award for Conscience and Integrity in Journalism from Nieman Foundation in the same year for covering politics and domestic abuse of Iranian women.

Shahla continues to highlight the needs and problems confronting Iranian women as an editor-in-chief of a new magazine called *Zanan-e-Emrooz* (*Today's Women*), which is published in print and online.

Art

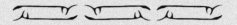

Arfa Atrae

Arfa Atrae (b. 1941) is an accomplished Santur musician and scholar of Persian music.

Atrae entered the Persian National Music Conservatory at the age of ten, and played for several national Iranian orchestras. She is the first woman to professionally teach Santur (dulcimer)—one of the most important Persian musical instruments—and is also a master of Radif, the complete repertoire of Persian traditional music.

In addition to her acclaimed concert appearances, she is an award-winning educator and has authored several books on practical and theoretical aspects of Iranian traditional music.

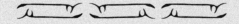

Fatemeh Motamed-Arya

Fatemeh Motamed-Arya (b. 1961), also known as Simin, is an award-winning actress and one of the most acclaimed figures of post-revolutionary Iranian cinema. She has been nominated nine times for the Best Actress Award at the Fajr International Film Festival, winning the top prize, the Crystal Simorgh, four times. Internationally, she won Best Actress at the Montreal World Film Festival in 2011 and was awarded France's Prix Henri Langlois in 2012, for her lifetime endeavours in the promotion of cinema and maintenance of professional cultural values.

Fatemeh is the first female member of the Board of Directors of House of Cinema, the Iranian Alliance of Motion Picture Guilds.

Forough Farrokhzad

Forough Farrokhzad (1934–1967) was one of the most influential contemporary Iranian poets. The first Iranian poet to freely express female desire and emotions, she was known as "The Rebel Poet of Iran" and introduced a new chapter in the history of Persian poetry. Forough, who studied to be a filmmaker, also directed a short documentary titled "The House Is Black" in 1962. Despite it being her only production, this film is considered a seminal work of the Iranian New Wave. She died at the age of 32 in a car accident.

To this day, Forough is still Iran's most well-known woman in Persian literature, and a cultural icon of modern Iran, inspiring many poets and artists across the world.

Googoosh

Googoosh (b. 1950), born Faegheh Atashin, is an amazing singer and actress and one of the most celebrated and enduring pop stars of Iran.

Before the Islamic Revolution, she starred in popular, blockbuster movies such as *Dar Emtedad-e Shab* (*Throughout the Night*) and *Hamsafar* (*Fellow Traveler*), and was at one point the most well-paid performing and recording artist in the country. After the Revolution, her career waned as women were no longer permitted to sing in public. Two decades later, Googoosh left Iran and restarted her music career abroad and continues to be a source of emulation and admiration for Iranian women.

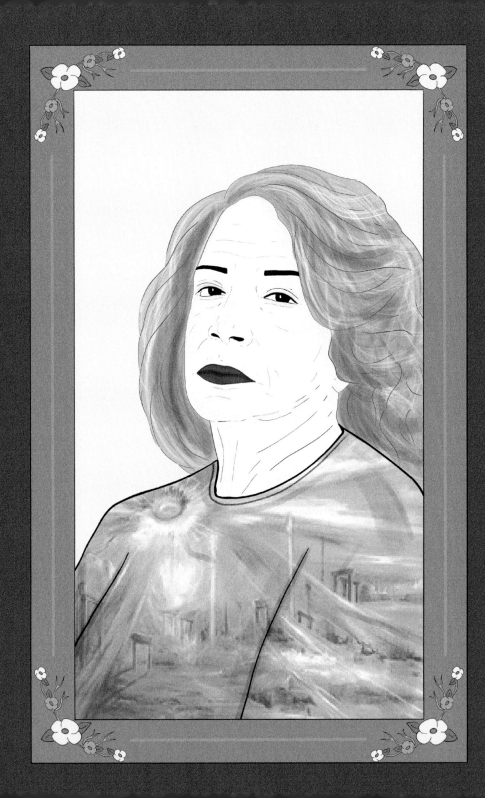

Iran Darroudi

Iran Darroudi (b. 1936), arguably the first contemporary female painter in Iran, is a renowned artist, art critic and director. In addition to her art critiques and lectures, she has held more than 60 individual exhibitions and 200 group exhibitions around the world, produced 80 collaborative documentaries, and written a best-selling autobiography entitled *In the Distance Between Two Points*.

In 2017, Iran was the first Iranian to receive the "Eternal Tile" on the wall of her house. The Eternal Tile is an award that is embedded onto the homes of 50 contemporary artists and literature figures by the Cultural Heritage, Tourism and Handicraft Organization of Iran, to celebrate the recipients as valuable representatives of national heritage.

Iran has donated 200 of her paintings to be put on permanent display at a foundation established in her name in Tehran, which when built will be the first private museum in Iranian history dedicated to a woman.

Jaleh Olov

Jaleh Olov (b. 1927) is a veteran actress, voice actress, narrator and poet. She started working in 1948 as a radio presenter and has since continued a longstanding career in radio, theatre and cinema. Jaleh is especially well-known for her dubbing of popular cartoons such as *Pinocchio* and *Sleeping Beauty*.

Among her many honours are lifetime achievement awards from Iran's House of Cinema in 2003, and the Iranian Artists Forum in 2018. She was also honoured by the Iranian Science and Culture Hall of Fame as one of the Everlasting Faces of Iran in 2010.

Lilit Teryan

Lilit (Liliet) Teryan (1930-2019) was a renowned sculptor, known as the "Mother of Sculpturing" in Iran. She was one of the first individuals to teach modern sculpture techniques in the country and was a founding member of the Faculty of Decorative Arts at the University of Tehran.

For many years after the Islamic Revolution of Iran, teaching sculpture was illegal and she was forced to teach in secrecy; in 1993, she resumed her work at the University.

Two of Lilit's most famous sculptures are a statue of Mesrop Mashtots, the founder of the Armenian alphabet, and of Yeprem Khan, an Iranian national hero.

Maryam Kazemzadeh

Maryam Kazemzadeh (b. 1956) is one of the relatively few female war photographers in the world.

Maryam was the first female photojournalist who tracked the Iran-Iraq War and she took care of injured soldiers even as she documented the conflict. Maryam's memoir, *War Photojournalist*, is about her experiences during the Islamic Revolution, the Iran-Iraq War and the years that followed.

Masoumeh Seyhoun

Masoumeh Seyhoun (1934–2010) was a painter. In 1974, she founded the Seyhoun Art Gallery, which is the oldest gallery in Iran and is notable for holding the first exhibitions of modern Iranian art.

Masoumeh introduced many talented young artists who later became leading figures in Iran's art scene such as Parviz Kalantari and Hossein Zenderoudi, and also created opportunities for self-taught artists such as Mokarrameh Ghanbari.

Mokarrameh Ghanbari

Mokarrameh Ghanbari (1928-2005) was a self-taught painter. Mokarrameh was an illiterate farmer who started painting at the age of 66 as a way to express her feelings. She painted on the walls of her home and appliances before starting to paint on paper. Her home, in the village of Darikandeh in Northern Iran, is now listed as a national heritage site.

Mokarrameh was introduced to the art world through her first exhibition at the Seyhoun Gallery in 1995. In 2001, she was honoured as the year's "Exemplary Woman" at the Conference of the Foundation of Iranian Women's Studies in Stockholm. In the same year, the Swedish National Museum named her "The Female Painter of 2001."

Monir Farmanfarmaian

Monir (Shahroudy) Farmanfarmaian (1922-2019) was a celebrated contemporary artist.

She received international acclaim for combining the traditional Iranian techniques of working with mirrors—"Aina-Kari"—with Western geometric abstraction. Her work has been shown in many museums and galleries around the world, such as the Museum of Modern Art and the Guggenheim Museum in New York and the Leighton House Museum in London. In 2015, Monir was named as one of the BBC's "100 Women."

In 2017, the Monir Museum, the first Iranian public museum dedicated entirely to honouring the work of a female artist opened in Tehran.

Pari Zanganeh

Pari Zanganeh (b. 1939) is a folkloric and operatic singer, educator and writer. Although she lost her eyesight in a car accident in 1971, she completed her studies in operatic music in Italy, Germany, and Austria and continued her career performing in major concert halls around the world.

Pari has won national and international achievements for her role in the restoration of traditional Persian music and in revitalizing and preserving regional folk songs. Her writings are diverse, encompassing songs, articles and books, the latter particularly for children. In her memoir, *Beyond Darkness*, she recounted her life experiences in order to raise awareness about the challenges of the blind.

Pari is also a United Nations Goodwill Ambassador, and has won the "International Gold Medal for Voice."

Qamar-ol-Moluk Vaziri

Qamar-ol-Moluk Vaziri (1905-1959), commonly known as her stage name "Qamar", was a mezzo-soprano, and in 1924 became the first woman in Iran to perform on a public stage in front of mixed audiences, men and women, without the obligatory hijab (veiling). She was also the first female recording artist of note, as well as the first female vocalist to sing and record political songs.

Qamar, known by many as "The Queen of Persian Music," was a role model for many Iranian female vocalists who followed her. She eventually stopped singing professionally in 1956, after over 30 years of working with popular songwriters and musicians.

Qamar was also a dedicated philanthropist, usually giving away the income from her concerts.

Rakhshan Banietemad

Rakhshan Banietemad (b. 1954) is a documentary maker, film director and screenwriter. She is known as one of the premier Iranian female filmmakers, and often explores societal and political issues, especially as they relate to women, in her films. In 1991, Rakhshan was the first woman to win the Best Director Award from the Fajr Film Festival, the most important such event in Iran.

In addition to many national and International awards, Rakhshan was awarded an honorary doctorate from SOAS University of London in 2008 in recognition of her body of work.

Rakhshan is a founder of KARA Film Studio, a group that produces and distributes documentaries about humanistic, societal and cultural issues. She has also been a Jury Member in international film festivals, such as the 2018 Mumbai International Film Festival, the 2017 Venice International Film Festival and 2017 American Academy Awards, Writers branch.

Simin Daneshvar

Simin Daneshvar (1921–2012) was a novelist, academic and translator, and an Iranian woman of many firsts. Her bestseller, *Savushun*, published in 1969, was the first modern novel in the Persian language written by a woman, and she was the first female writer whose works were translated from Persian to English.

Before writing her novel, Simin was also the first Iranian woman to publish a short story collection under her own name in 1948 and was elected as the first chair of the Iranian Writers Union in 1968.

Shirin Neshat

Shirin Neshat (b. 1957) is a renowned contemporary visual artist who employs photography, video installation, cinema and performance to explore the relationship between women, religious and political structures in Iran and other Middle Eastern societies.

Shirin's works have been shown in many solo exhibitions at museums and galleries internationally. Among her many awards: she won the First International Prize at the 48th Venice Biennale (1999), the Hiroshima Freedom Prize (2005), the Dorothy and Lillian Gish Prize (2006) and the Praemium Imperiale award for her lifetime achievement (2017). In 2010, Shirin was also named "Artist of the Decade" by The Huffington Post. In 2009, her first feature-length film, *Women Without Men*, received the Silver Lion Award for Best Director at the 66th Venice International Film Festival. Her film, *Looking for Oum Kulthum*, was screened at the Toronto Film Festival in 2017. In the same year, Shirin directed Giuseppe Verdi's opera *Aida* at the Salzburg Festival.

Education

Jaleh Amouzegar

Jaleh Amouzegar (b. 1939) is a renowned linguist, university professor and scholar of ancient Iranian languages and culture. As an educator and researcher, she played a significant role in furthering ancient Iranian studies and the history of literature in ancient Iran and has written several books and articles in Persian, English and French.

Jaleh has received numerous national and international awards, including the International Society of Iranian Studies Lifetime Achievement Award in 2010, and in 2016, both the Chevalier of the Legion of Honor, the highest decoration awarded by the French government, and the Persian Cypress Award, an Iranian Cultural Heritage prize.

Noushafarin Ansari

Noushafarin Ansari (b. 1938) is an educator, librarian and retired university professor. She has garnered widespread recognition for her seminal role in developing and organizing the Children's Book Council (CBC), a non-governmental and non-profit organization for cultural and research activities in the field of children's literature.

As the founder and leader of the International Board of Books for Young People (IBBY) in Iran, Noushafarin was a keynote speaker at the 28th IBBY Congress in 2002, and named as an Honorary Member of IBBY in 2010.

Parirokh Dadsetan

Parirokh Dadsetan (1933-2010) was a psychologist and university professor highly acknowledged for her work in transformational psychology. At sixteen years of age, Parirokh was the only woman to win a government scholarship to study in Switzerland under the supervision of Jean Piaget, one of the most prominent psychologists of the 20th century.

Parirokh wrote several books and articles in Persian and English, and her *Psychopathology from Childhood to Adolescence* was selected as the Book of the Year by The Islamic Republic of Iran in 1993.

In addition to many other awards, Parirokh was honoured in 2002 by the Iranian Science and Culture Hall of Fame as one of the Everlasting Faces of Iran. She also won the Kharazmi International Award in 2005 for her outstanding research in the human sciences.

Qamar Ariyan

Qamar Ariyan (1922-2012) was a researcher and author, and one of the first women to graduate from the Faculty of Literature at Tehran University, as well as one of the country's first female university professors.

Qamar was also an influential academic of Iranian culture who published many significant articles and books, and received widespread attention for writing *The Image of Christ in Persian Literature*, one of the most important books on the impact of Christianity on Persian literature. Qamar was also a member of the Supreme Council of the Great Islamic Encyclopedia.

Roza Mantazemi

Roza Mantazemi, born Fatemeh Bahrayni, (1921-2009) was a cooking teacher and author one of the most famous cookbooks in Iran.

Her comprehensive work *The Art of Cooking* (in Persian: *Honar-e Aashpazi*) has been in publication since 1964. The first edition of the book included 600 Iranian and non-Iranian recipes and today there are more than 50 published editions with over 1700 recipes.

Art of Cooking remained a best-seller in Iran for over 50 years and was considered a wartime essential during the Iran-Iraq war, despite publishing issues such as paper shortages.

Tajzaman Danesh

Tajzaman Danesh (1926- 2009) was a law scholar and university lecturer. After receiving her PhD in Criminal Law and Penalty Law, Tajzaman compiled the first scientific manual about prisons for the Iranian judicial system. She was the first Iranian to suggest that juveniles should go through a separate prison and court system, and she established the first educational workshops for prison inmates.

Tajzaman had an active speaking career on issues related to incarceration at national and international conferences and published numerous articles on the same subject in international law journals. A number of her books are used as essential reference works in Iranian universities.

Touran Mirhadi

Touran Mirhadi (1927–2016) was a pioneer of modern education and children's literature.

Touran was the founder of the Farhad School, an experimental and innovative educational complex established in the 1955, and also held the first children's book exhibition in Iran in 1957. She is especially renowned as the co-founder of the Children's Book Council (CBC) of Iran and the Encyclopedia for Young People (EYP). The former is one of the most prominent organizations in children's literature in Iran, providing a platform for Iranian children's books to gain international exposure. The EYP project started on a largely voluntary basis in 1980 with the collaboration of many editorial and youth advisory groups in response to the need for a reliable reference book for young Iranians. During her lifetime, thirteen volumes of the encyclopedia were completed.

Despite several tragic incidents during her life, she lived by the motto that one ought to "turn a great sorrow into great work."

Entrepreneurship & Philanthropy

Ashraf Bahadorzadeh

Ashraf (Ghandehari) Bahadorzadeh (1925-2017) was a social entrepreneur who dedicated her life to challenge the prejudiced perceptions of elderly and disabled people and to empower them to become active members of society.

Through her Modern Kahrizak Charity Foundation, Ashraf transformed the Kahrizak hospice into a world-class, advanced nonprofit organization to take care of Iran's disabled and elderly, free of charge, and organized many charity fairs and fundraising bazaars in Iran and abroad.

Ashraf also co-founded the Ladies Charitable Society (LCS) NGO in 1973 to coordinate philanthropic efforts to support Kahrizak's patients and other vulnerable people in Iran.

Farangis Yeganegi

Farangis Yeganegi (Shahrokh) (1916-2010), was the founder and organizer of many socio-religious, rehabilitative and cultural organizations in Iran. Farangis was the creator and the first executive manager of the Iranian Handicraft Organization, and was also one of the founders and the first chairperson of The High Council of Iranian Women.

Farangis founded the Zoroastrian Women's Organization as well as the Ancient Iranian Culture Association, for which she built a library named after her late husband, the Ardeshir Yeganegi Library. She dedicated her life to improving the standard of living for many neglected segments of society such as orphans, female prisoners, craftsmen, Zoroastrians and women.

Narges Kalbasi

Narges Kalbasi Ashtari (b. 1988) is a humanitarian and aid worker.

Orphaned as a child, Narges lived with her aunt in Canada. In 2011, she established the Prishan Foundation, an orphanage for girls, in Rayagada, India. She later founded another home for blind children in Mukundapur.

In 2017, Narges moved back to Iran to offer humanitarian aid to those affected by the devastating earthquake in Kermanshah. The following year she established Yaraan-e-Eshgh, an NGO that focuses on philanthropic activities for a variety of causes, and was honoured as the public figure of the year (voted by viewers) by *Formool Yek*, a popular Iranian TV show.

Saeedeh Ghods

Saeedeh Ghods (b. 1951) is a philanthropist, best known as the founder of Mahak, a non-profit, non-governmental society to support children suffering from cancer. In addition to managing Mahak, which is now the largest specialized centre for the treatment of children's cancer in the Middle East, Saeedeh is a founding member of the Breast Cancer Society of Iran, The International Society for Children with Cancer and the Green Front of Iran organization.

Saeedeh won the 2008 Islamic Development Bank (IDB) prize given to Muslim women for their achievements and contributions in development, for her work and efforts to improve children's healthcare. She also was named in *The Wall Street Journal*'s 2008 "Top 50 Women to Watch."

Saeedeh also wrote the award-winning book *Kimia Khatun*, the story of Rumi's step-daughter.

Sattareh Farmanfarmaian

Sattareh Farmanfarmaian (1921-2012) was the founder of the Tehran School of Social Work and a pioneer of family planning in Iran.

The daughter of AbdolHossein Mirza Farmanfarmaian, a prince of the Qajar dynasty, Sattareh used her family's influence to establish social welfare associations, modern daycare and healthcare centres to serve orphans, hospital patients and prostitutes.

In 1992, Sattareh published her widely-read autobiography *Daughter of Persia: A Woman's Journey from Her Father's Harem Through the Islamic Revolution* which was nominated for a Pulitzer Prize.

Shahindokht Sarlati

Shahindokht Sarlati (1933-2004), is known for her work in the fields of entrepreneurship and philanthropy. She transformed the agriculture of Lalehzaar region of Kerman, Iran, by replacing fields of poppies (which generated opium) with roses. She also changed the lives of local farmers by offering them educational support and monetary assistance.

In 1978, Shahindokht and her husband, Homayoun Sanati, established the Zahra Rosewater Company, the leading Iranian producer and exporter of rosewater and rose oil. As the first supplier of organically produced floral products, Zahra Company produces more than five percent of the world's rose oil.

Shahindokht also helped organize the Sanati Foundation, a charity devoted to promoting social, educational and cultural development, which has aided more than 250 disadvantaged children and orphans.

Zinat Daryaie

Zinat Daryaie (b. 1968) is an entrepreneur and healthcare worker. As a member of a traditional society in a small village of Qeshm Island in southern Iran, Zinat was the first woman to remove her face veil (Boregheh), to work as a midwife and healthcare worker. Despite societal resistance, Zinat ran in the first local elections after the Islamic Revolution and secured a council seat, winning with the most votes.

Besides her other environmental and entrepreneurial activities, Zinat has developed her village into a popular tourism hub, attracting many travellers from around the world. In addition to creating job opportunities for over two hundred people—especially the women of Qeshm Island—she has positively impacted the area's eco-tourism.

Science

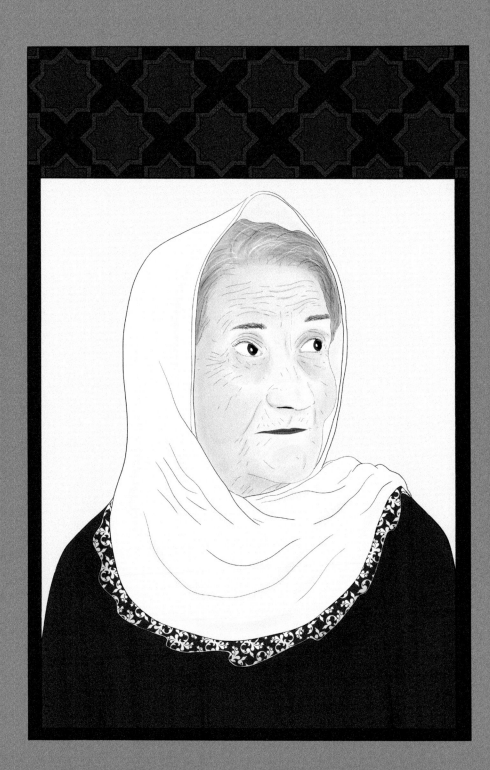

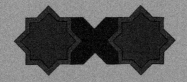

Alenoush Terian

Alenoush Terian (1921-2011), known as the "Mother of Modern Iranian Astronomy," was the first female physics professor at the University of Tehran and the first female astronomer in Iran. She was also one of the founders of the solar telescopic observatory of the Institute of Geophysics at the University of Tehran, where she worked until her retirement.

Maryam Mirzakhani

Maryam Mirzakhani (1977–2017) was a distinguished mathematician and a professor of mathematics at Stanford University. Maryam's long list of accolades dated back to 1994, when at the age of 17, she became the first female Iranian student to win a gold medal in the Hong Kong International Mathematical Olympiad. She was also the first to achieve a perfect score and won two gold medals the following year in the Toronto International Mathematical Olympiad.

Most notably, in 2014, she was the first Iranian as well as the first woman to win the Fields Medal, known as the Nobel Prize of Mathematics. Maryam passed away at the age of 40 and in 2018, in honour of her achievements, her birthday (May 12) was selected to mark Celebration of Women in Mathematics Day internationally.

Mina Izadyar

Mina Izadyar (1949-2013) was a hematologist-oncologist and prominent university professor. She was the Founder and Chairwoman of the Iranian Thalassemia Society. Owing to her efforts, cases of infants with acute thalassemia in Iran reduced significantly and Iran became the first developing country leading the fight against this disease. Mina was also co-founder of the Iranian Pediatric Hematology-Oncology Society and the head of the Hematology-and-Oncology Ward at Children's Medical Center, affiliated with the Tehran University of Medical Sciences.

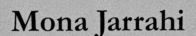

Mona Jarrahi

Mona Jarrahi (b. 1979) is a professor of electrical engineering at the University of California, Los Angeles (UCLA).

In 2013, Mona became the first Iranian to receive the Presidential Early Career Award for Scientists and Engineers, the highest honour of its kind bestowed by the United States, for her research on Terahertz Optoelectronics. Mona has received several other prestigious awards for her outstanding achievements including the Burroughs Wellcome Fund's Innovations in Regulatory Science Award, Early Career Award from the National Science Foundation, Okawa Foundation Research Award and Sharif University of Technology Distinguished Alumni Award.

Nasrin Moazami

Nasrin Moazami (b. 1945) is a microbiologist, university professor and a pioneer in biofuel technology in Iran. In 1987, Nasrin founded a research centre that is acknowledged to be Iran's best-equipped biotechnology lab and the only Regional Reference Center for Biotechnology in West and Central Asia. In 1995, she established Iran's first institute for applied marine biotechnology. In 2015, she was appointed to the Scientific Board of the International Basic Sciences Program (IBSP) of UNESCO.

Among many other national and international awards, in 1995 she received the Chevalier de I'Orde des Palmes Academiques, a national order bestowed by France for her outstanding professional research.

Nectar Papazian

Nectar Papazian-Andreef (b. 1927) was among the first generation of women architects who studied at the Faculty of Fine Arts at the University of Tehran. In 1945, she became the first Iranian woman with a graduate diploma in architecture.

Nectar was also the first woman to be involved in the projects of the Ministry of Housing and Urban Planning and has made many contributions in planning comprehensive educational institutions in Iran. Her major projects include rendering the master plans of Jondi Shahpour and Pahlavi (Shiraz) Universities, as well as the master plan of the city of Tabriz, and planning for several student residences and centres for technical training in Iran.

Parvaneh Vossough

Parvaneh Vossough (1935-2013) was a pediatric hematologist-oncologist who established the first pediatric hemato-oncology ward in a children's hospital in Iran.

Parvaneh was the chairperson of the Board of Trustees of Mahak, a charity foundation supporting children with cancer and later, she became the chief physician of Mahak hospital. Following her death, the City Council of Tehran changed the name of a street near Mahak to Vossough Street in honour of her lifelong contributions to the community.

Parvaneh, known by many as "Iran's Mother Teresa," was an active member of various international medical societies and published more than a hundred papers in various medical journals.

Zahra Alizadeh Sani

Zahra Alizadeh Sani (b. 1973) is an award-winning cardiologist and Associate Professor of Cardiology, who has played a key role in establishing advanced Cardiac MRI (CMR) capabilities in Iran.

In addition to the many academic articles she has published on the subject, she is a founding member of the Iranian chapter of the International Society of Magnetic Resonance in Medicine and Iran's representative on the Executive Committee of the Asian Society of Cardiovascular Imaging. She created the first Cardiac MRI department in Iran and was awarded a special gold medal as the best world woman inventor by the Board of Referees of the Geneva International Festival for Inventions, and was also noted as the best case presenter at the Euro CMR in 2014.

Sport

Fereshteh Karimi

Fereshteh Karimi (b. 1989) is a well-regarded player for the Iranian women's national futsal team.

In 2013, Fereshteh, known as the "Queen of Asian Futsal," was chosen as one of the top ten nominees for the best female player in the world by the FutsalPlanet website. In 2015, she won the first AFC Women's Futsal Championship (Asian Champions League) playing for Iran and was chosen as the Most Valuable Player of the tournament. She was also the Most Valuable Player of the 2018 AFC tournament.

Kimia Alizadeh

Kimia Alizadeh (b. 1998) is a Taekwondo athlete.

Kimia won a bronze medal at the 2016 Summer Olympics and became the first Iranian woman to win a medal in the Olympics. She also won a gold medal at the Nanjing 2014 Youth Olympic Games, as well as a bronze medal and a silver medal at the 2015 and 2017 Taekwondo World Championships, respectively. In 2019, Kimia was listed in BBC's "100 Women" as an athlete inspiring the next generation of Iranian women in martial arts.

As of this writing, Kimia has announced that she will no longer compete for Iran because of the constraints women face in that country. Prior to the postponement of worldwide sporting events due to the coronavirus, she indicated that she was contemplating representing Germany, her current place of residence, at the 2020 Summer Olympics.

Laleh Seddigh

Laleh Seddigh (b. 1977) is a professional female race car driver. Laleh has made her mark in Iranian sports history by competing and winning in a male-dominated sport and is also the first Iranian woman since the 1979 Islamic Revolution who has been allowed to compete against men.

Laleh, nicknamed "little Schumacher," has an International Racing Driving License and is allowed to race globally. She is now an official member of the coaching committee of the Iranian Automobile Federation and is training a new generation of female and male race drivers.

Maryam Tousi

Maryam Tousi (b. 1988) is the first Iranian to win a gold medal as a sprinter in 400m at the 2012 Asian Indoor Championships. She is known as "the fastest girl of Iran" and is the record holder of the country's 100m, 200m, and 400m races.

Parvaneh Kazemi

Parvaneh Kazemi (b. 1970), a mathematics teacher, is the first Iranian female mountaineer to independently attempt Mount Everest, the highest mountain above sea level on Earth.

Parvaneh is also the first woman in the world to summit both Mount Everest and Mount Lhotse, the fourth highest peak on earth, in a single week.

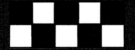

Sara Khadem

Sara Khadem (Khademalsharieh) (b. 1997) is a professional chess player and the first Woman International Master of Iran. Sara won her first international major title at the age of 12 as the third Iranian to have won that title. Sara has played and won many national and international championships since then and now holds the titles of Woman FIDE (The Fédération Internationale des Échecs) Master (2008), Woman International Master (2011), Woman Grandmaster (2013) and International Master (2015).

As of this writing, Sara is ranked 14 among the top 100 female players at FIDE, International Chess Federation.

Susan Rashidi

Susan (Sahar) Rashidi (b. 1992) is a kickboxing champion. As a Kurdish Iranian raised in a nomadic tribe in the Kermanshah province of northwest Iran, Susan has had to combat traditional strictures again female participation in sports. She has won eleven national championships and was among the top Iranian sportswomen of 2017.

She continues to fight such stereotypes for herself and others and has established a tent-based "sports club" to teach kickboxing to the girls of her tribe.

Zahra Nemati

Zahra Nemati (b. 1985) is a Paralympic and Olympic archer. Zahra was a black belt in Taekwondo before a car accident in 2004 left her with a spinal cord injury. In 2006, she started learning archery and quickly became a medalist and world record breaker in national and international archery and Para archery championships. Winning two medals at 2012 London Summer Paralympics, Zahra became the first Iranian woman to win a gold medal at both the Olympic and Paralympic Games.

Zahra, who carried the Iranian flag during the Opening Ceremony of the 2016 Olympic Games in Rio de Janeiro, is a two-time Paralympic champion and a two-time world champion and the only Paralympian to compete at the Olympic Games in the same year.

Her other achievements include an individual award at the SportAccord Spirit of Sport Awards in St. Petersburg, Russia in 2013, given to athletes who have made exceptional and lasting positive social change through sports.

Acknowledgments

This book couldn't be published without the kindness of many people.

Special thanks to:

Hossein, my husband, for giving me the courage to illustrate and write this book and for being beside me in all stages of the book's preparation.

My dad, mom and brother, Mahsa Jelveh, Afsaneh Salari, Mariam Neza, Maryam and my other friends and family members for showing confidence in my work and for their support.

All amazing scholars who helped me to select these 50 inspiring women.

Shayan Khaksar for proofreading the very first draft of the book.

Khaleh Zohreh, Aida Mofakham of The Blooming Apples, Shadi, Leyla, and other incredible supporters for their generous donations.

My Kickstarter campaign's backers for believing in this book.

And last but not least, my deepest gratitude to Mandana Chaffa, my remarkable editor, for her invaluable contribution and insightful suggestions.